THE LITTLE GREEN BOOK OF

MOTHERS' WISDOM

THE LITTLE GREEN BOOK OF

MOTHERS' WISDOM

Edited by Carissa Bonham

Skyhorse Publishing

Skyhorse Publishing books may be purchased in bulk at special discounts for sales promotion, corporate gifts, fund-raising, or educational purposes. Special editions can also be created to specifications. For details, contact the Special Sales Department, Skyhorse Publishing, 307 West 36th Street, 11th Floor, New York, NY 10018 or info@skyhorsepublishing.com.

Skyhorse® and Skyhorse Publishing® are registered trademarks of Skyhorse Publishing, Inc.®, a Delaware corporation.

Visit our website at www.skyhorsepublishing.com.

10 9 8 7 6 5 4 3 2 1

Library of Congress Cataloging-in-Publication Data is available on file.

Cover design by Daniel Brount
Cover photo credit: Getty Images

Print ISBN: 978-1-5107-5602-1
Ebook ISBN: 978-1-5107-5603-8

Printed in China

To the fierce mama bears who found their voices and fought for their families in the face of corruption.

Contents

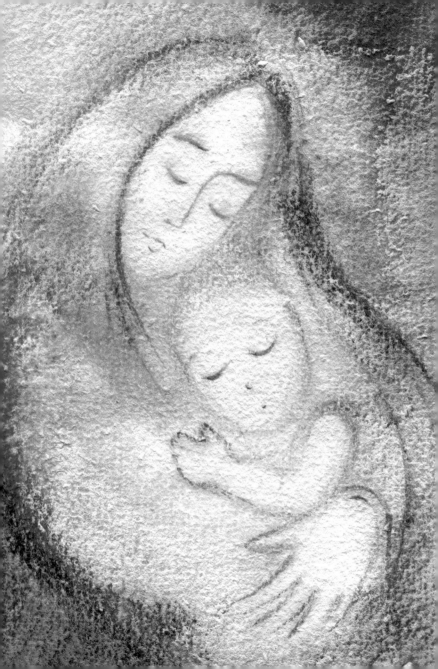

Introduction

Becoming a mother was an earth-shattering, transformative experience for me. This was only enhanced, of course, by all the hurdles that stood in my way. I lost my first four pregnancies to miscarriage. When I unintentionally became pregnant a fifth time, my baby didn't have a heartbeat and the doctor told me it wasn't viable. Whether it was God's whisper or my budding mother's intuition, something inside me wasn't ready to give up.

Despite my doctor's skepticism, two weeks later, my baby did have a heartbeat. That little "not viable" life grew and grew and was born three weeks early—weighing in at more than ten pounds—on Mother's Day. The little miracle baby boy that first made me a mom is now a healthy and happy nine-year-old.

When he was born, my heart unfolded like an intricate piece of origami, to reveal new areas, sections, and compartments that I never knew existed. My capacity to love became greater than I could have ever imagined. It was like I hadn't quite fully been able to become myself until I became a mom.

I now have a second little boy, as well, and being a mom feels like one of the most important things I could be doing for today's society. The world needs more kind, smart, compassionate, capable people. I know I'm not the only one raising young kids today who feels the weight of the important role that mothers play in society as we raise more of the kinds of people that it needs.

So what makes this book green?

When Skyhorse approached me about writing a new book for their Little Red Books series with quotes about motherhood, I was excited. But I also asked what they might think about making it a little *green* book.

As a green lifestyle writer for *Creative Green Living* (www .creativegreenliving.com), my approach to life is distinctly *green* and that also affects how I approach motherhood. I care about toxins, sustainability, and waste. I breastfed, babywore, and practiced attachment parenting. I had a doula, a water birth, and used cloth diapers. I believe I can make better medical choices for my baby (with advice from my doctor, of course) than any one-size-fits-all government program.

So, some of the things that are attached to the way I approach motherhood are going to ooze out onto these pages.

Not feeling so green yourself? We still have more in common as moms than you might realize. While you might not find that every quote resonates with you, I think you'll find quite a few (the vast majority, even) that tug on your soul a little bit as they describe your own experience with motherhood.

My hope is that no matter who you are or how green you feel, you'll find quotes about motherhood in here that you love, that will remind you why you became a mom in the first place, and that you'll love enough to share.

About the quotes you'll find here

I've done my best to find the best quotes possible—both by mothers and about mothers. Not everyone quoted is a mother themselves. There are several quotes by men or women who are not mothers about the profound impact mothers have and I found them insightful enough to share.

I'd also like to take this moment to recognize that history and humans are complicated. Quotes appear here based on their stand-alone merits and do not necessarily imply an endorsement of the person or other viewpoints a quoted individual might hold.

I hope you enjoy this book and find nuggets of truth to inspire you!

—Carissa Bonham

The Journey to Motherhood

"Having a child flips your concept of love upside down into new depths, otherwise unknown to the human heart."
—JULIEANNE O'CONNOR

• • •

"I didn't lose myself when I became a mom.
I found a new and better version of me."
—ALEXIS ROBINSON

• • •

"Little souls find their way to you, whether they're from your womb or someone else's."
—SHERYL CROW

• • •

"It is important to keep in mind that our bodies must work pretty well, or there wouldn't be so many humans on the planet."
—INA MAY GASKIN, *INA MAY'S GUIDE TO CHILDBIRTH*

• • •

"Having children just puts the whole world into perspective. Everything else just disappears."
—KATE WINSLET

• • •

"All those clichés—those things you hear about having a baby and motherhood—all of them are true. And all of them are the most beautiful things you will ever experience."
—PENELOPE CRUZ

• • •

"Completeness? Happiness? These words don't come close to describing my emotions. There truly is nothing I can say to capture what motherhood means to me, particularly given my medical history."
—ANITA BAKER

• • •

"Being a mother is an attitude, not a biological relation."
—ROBERT A. HEINLEIN, *HAVE SPACE SUIT—WILL TRAVEL*

• • •

"Who is this angel, sent here to change me,
sent here to take me where I've never been?
Long I have wandered, weary and waiting,
for something to shake me and life to begin."
—"THIS ANGEL" BY JENNIFER NETTLES

• • •

"Giving birth does not make her a mother.
Placing a child for adoption does not make her less of one."
—UNKNOWN

• • •

"You instantly become less selfish. You can't be the
biggest person in the world anymore—they are.
Motherhood really grounds you."
—KERI RUSSELL

• • •

"This mothering role will teach you more about
yourself than you ever expected."
—TRICIA GOYER, *TEEN MOM: YOU'RE STRONGER
THAN YOU THINK*

• • •

"Becoming a mother makes you the mother of all children.
From now on each wounded, abandoned, frightened child is
yours. You live in the suffering mothers of every race and creed
and weep with them. You long to comfort all who are desolate."
—CHARLOTTE GRAY

• • •

"Some say that pregnancy make a woman an instant mother. To
that I say, I became an instant woman the day I became a mother."
—EFRAT CYBULKIEWICZ

• • •

"There is such a special sweetness in being
able to participate in creation."
—PAMELA S. NADAV

• • •

"A child born to another woman calls me Mom. The depth of the
tragedy and the magnitude of the privilege are not lost on me."
—JODY LANDERS

• • •

"I believe the choice to become a mother is the choice to become
one of the greatest spiritual teachers there is."
—OPRAH WINFREY

• • •

"Giving birth and being born brings us into the essence of creation, where the human spirit is courageous and bold, and the body, a miracle of wisdom."
—HARRIETTE HARTIGAN

• • •

"[Motherhood is] the biggest gamble in the world. It is the glorious life force. It's huge and scary—it's an act of infinite optimism."
—GILDA RADNER

• • •

"I have found being a mother has made me emotionally raw in many situations. Your heart is beating outside your body when you have a baby."
—KATE BECKINSALE

• • •

"Motherhood is more awesome than I ever thought it could be
and harder than I ever would have imagined."
—SARAH WILLIAMS, *CUPCAKES ON A TUESDAY*

● ● ●

"The moment a child is born, the mother is also born.
She never existed before."
—RAJNEESH

● ● ●

"When the whole world made me think that,
I can't do it,
Thanks for making me, believe that,
I can do it."
—LUFFINA LOURDURAJ

● ● ●

"Motherhood: All love begins and ends there."
—ROBERT BROWNING

• • •

"Motherhood definitely isn't an easy job, but it's the best job
there is, I wouldn't trade it for the world."
—BIANCA MILLAR, *A TRIBE CALLED BEAUTY*

• • •

"The parenting process forces moms and dads to mature
in a way no other life experience can."
—GARY EZZO AND DR. ROBERT BUCKNAM,
ON BECOMING PRETEEN WISE

• • •

"Motherhood is heart-exploding, blissful hysteria."
— OLIVIA WILDE

• • •

"I thought I knew the depth of love I was capable of before becoming a mother. But giving birth unlocked areas of my heart I never knew existed and made my capacity to love so much greater."
—CARISSA BONHAM

• • •

"Whether your pregnancy was meticulously planned, medically coaxed, or happened by surprise, one thing is certain—your life will never be the same."
—CATHERINE JONES

• • •

"A miracle is really the only way to describe motherhood and giving birth. It's unbelievable how God has made us women and babies to endure and be able to do so much. A miracle indeed. Such an incredible blessing."
—JENNIE FINCH

• • •

"Motherhood is a million little moments that God weaves together with grace, redemption, laughter, tears and most of all, love."
—LYSA TERKEURST

• • •

"Giving birth should be your greatest achievement, not your greatest fear."
—JANE WEIDEMAN, DOULA

• • •

"There are times when the adoption process
is exhausting and painful and makes you want to scream.
But . . . so does childbirth."
—Scott Simon

• • •

"As it stands, motherhood is a sort of wilderness through which
each woman hacks her way, part martyr, part pioneer; a turn of
events from which some women derive feelings of heroism, while
others experience a sense of exile from the world they knew."
—Rachel Cusk

• • •

"Being a mother means that your heart is no longer yours;
it wanders wherever your children do."
—George Bernard Shaw

• • •

"Pregnancy and motherhood are the most beautiful and significantly life-altering events that I have ever experienced."
—ELISABETH HASSELBECK

• • •

"Adoption is when a child grew in its mommy's heart instead of her tummy."
—UNKNOWN

• • •

"The natural state of motherhood is unselfishness. When you become a mother, you are no longer the center of your own universe. You relinquish that position to your children."
—JESSICA LANGE

• • •

"Biology is the least of what makes someone a mother."
—OPRAH WINFREY

• • •

"Having kids—the responsibility of rearing good, kind, ethical, responsible human beings—is the biggest job anyone can embark on."
—MARIA SHRIVER

• • •

"However motherhood comes to you, it's a miracle."
—VALERIE HARPER

• • •

"A mother's love for her child is like no other love.
To be able to put that feeling aside because you want the
best for your child is the most unselfish thing I know."
—MARY, A BIRTH MOTHER, ON ADOPTION

• • •

"Family is not defined by our genes,
it is built and maintained through love."
—AMALIA G

• • •

"Birth is the epicenter of women's power."
—ANI DIFRANCO

• • •

"The bond that links your true family is not one of blood,
but of respect and joy in each other's life."
—RICHARD BACH

• • •

"Motherhood is the greatest thing and the hardest thing."
—RICKI LAKE

• • •

"Somehow destiny comes into play. These children end up with
you and you end up with them. It's something quite magical."
—NICOLE KIDMAN

2

The Life-Giving Power of Mothers

"Adam named his wife Eve, because she would
become the mother of all the living."
—Genesis 3:20, New International Version

• • •

"My birth mother brought me into this world,
but it was my adoptive parents who gave me life."
—Christina Romo

• • •

"She is the creature of life, the giver of life,
and the giver of abundant love, care, and protection.
Such are the great qualities of a mother."
—AMA H.VANNIARACHCHY

• • •

"Mother-love is the great, surging, divine current that plays
forever through humanity."
—ELBERT HUBBARD

• • •

"Practice. Patience at every step of the way—you will
never regret how patient you were with your children."
—TAMARA RUBIN, LEAD SAFE MAMA, AWARD WINNING
ENVIRONMENTAL ACTIVIST AND DOCUMENTARY FILMMAKER

• • •

"Your children need to have a cushion to fall on.
That cushion is you. That cushion is love."
—CAROLINA KING, *MAMA INSTINCTS*

• • •

"You're always going to wonder if you're doing things wrong, but
that's what it means to be a mom, to care so much about someone
else that you just want to be as perfect as possible."
—NAYA RIVERA

• • •

"My mother's love has always been a sustaining force for our
family, and one of my greatest joys is seeing her integrity, her
compassion, her intelligence reflected in my daughters."
—MICHELLE OBAMA

• • •

"There is no greater good in all the world than
motherhood. The influence of a mother in the lives
of her children is beyond calculation."
—JAMES E. FAUST

• • •

"Breastfeeding reminds us of the universal truth of abundance;
the more we give out, the more we are filled up, and that divine
nourishment—the source from which we all draw—is, like a
mother's breast, ever full and ever flowing."
— SARAH BUCKLEY

• • •

"No matter what, a mother always loves her children."
—CATHERINE PULSIFER

• • •

"A mother's happiness is like a beacon, lighting up the future but reflected also on the past in the guise of fond memories."
—HONORE DE BALZAC

• • •

"When little people are overwhelmed by big emotions, it's our job to share our calm, not to join their chaos."
—L. R. KNOST

• • •

"The bond between mothers and their children is one defined by love. As a mother's prayers for her children are unending, so are the wisdom, grace, and strength they provide to their children."
—PRESIDENT GEORGE W. BUSH

• • •

"'Dreams, passion, and don't get eaten by a shark,' a father's last words, delivered to my marine-biologist daughter at the BLUE ocean conference. So, we embarked on a life-giving road trip: crying, screaming from mountain tops, skiing pure sunshine, sitting on Maine's rocky coast, remembering another father quote: 'Life, you can't live without it.'"
—KRISTINE AKINS, ENTREPRENEUR AND CREATOR OF CHARLIECURLS

• • •

"There is no other organ quite like the uterus. If men had such an organ they would brag about it. So should we."
—INA MAY GASKIN, AUTHOR OF SPIRITUAL MIDWIFERY

• • •

"The way we talk to our children becomes their inner voice."
—PEGGY O'MARA, AUTHOR OF NATURAL FAMILY LIVING

• • •

"In giving birth to our babies, we may find that we give birth to new possibilities within ourselves."
—MYLA KABAT-ZINN

• • •

"I learned from my mother that there is a greatness in all of us, and that all of us are delivered to this world with a mission."
—LES BROWN, *LIVE YOUR DREAMS*

• • •

"Love as powerful as your mother's for you leaves its own mark. To have been loved so deeply, even though the person who loved us is gone, will give us some protection forever."
—(DUMBLEDORE TO HARRY POTTER) *HARRY POTTER & THE PHILOSOPHER'S STONE* BY J. K. ROWLING

• • •

"Perhaps the reason we respond so universally to our mothers'
love is because it typifies the love of our Savior."
—BRADLEY D. FOSTER

● ● ●

"The only thing I ever had was you, it's true;
And even when the times got hard you were there
to let us know that we'd get through."
—"THANK YOU MOM" BY GOOD CHARLOTTE

● ● ●

"The heart of a mother is a deep abyss at the bottom of which you
will always find forgiveness."
—HONORE DE BALZAC

● ● ●

"But the most important thing I learned from Mom is that nothing is more precious or sacred than doing God's will."
—KENNETH W. HAGIN

• • •

"Only God Himself fully appreciates the influence of a Christian mother in the molding of character in her children."
—BILLY GRAHAM

• • •

"The best part of being a mom to me is the unconditional love. I have never felt a love as pure, a love that's as rewarding."
—MONICA DENISE BROWN

• • •

"Mother's milk is soul food for babies. The babies of
the world need a lot more soul food."
— INA MAY GASKIN, *INA MAY'S GUIDE TO BREASTFEEDING*

• • •

"The wisdom and compassion a woman can intuitively
experience in childbirth can make her a source of healing
and understanding for other women."
—STEPHEN GASKIN, HUSBAND OF INA MAY GASKIN AND
COFOUNDER OF THE FARM

• • •

"It is easier to build strong children than to repair broken adults."
—FREDERICK DOUGLASS

• • •

"The highest and noblest work in this life is that of a mother."
—RUSSELL M. NELSON

• • •

"Who is it that loves me and will love me forever with an affection which no chance, no misery, no crime of mine can do away? It is you, my mother."
—THOMAS CARLYLE

• • •

"You taught me to run, you taught me to fly, helped me to free the me inside."
— "MUSIC OF MY HEART"
BY GLORIA ESTEFAN AND *NSYNC

• • •

"Just as a woman's heart knows how and when to pump, her lungs to inhale, and her hand to pull back from fire, so she knows when and how to give birth."
—VIRGINIA DIORIO

• • •

"To your baby, you are the best mother."
—DR. WILLIAM SEARS, *THE ATTACHMENT PARENTING BOOK*

• • •

"Birth is not only about making babies. Birth is about making mothers — strong, competent, capable mothers who trust themselves and know their inner strength."
—BARBARA KATZ ROTHMAN,
AUTHOR OF *A BUN IN THE OVEN*

• • •

"No gift to your mother can ever equal her gift to you—life."
—UNKNOWN

• • •

"Birth is the sudden opening of a window,
through which you look out upon a stupendous
prospect. For what has happened? A miracle. You have
exchanged nothing for the possibility of everything."
—WILLIAM MACNEILE DIXON

• • •

"I remember my mother's prayers and they have always
followed me. They have clung to me all my life."
—ABRAHAM LINCOLN

• • •

"I know of no better answer to [the] foul practices that
confront our young people than the teachings of a mother,
given in love with an unmistakable warning."
—GORDON B. HINCKLEY

• • •

"Having such a supportive and encouraging mom
has been a big part of my success."
—VERN YIP

• • •

"You've given me everything that I will need to
make it through this crazy thing called life."
— "MAMA'S SONG" BY CARRIE UNDERWOOD

• • •

"How you parent your kids today is shaping who they will be as adults and it's shaping their internal voice."
—Carolina King, *Mama Instincts*

• • •

"A mother's love is patient and forgiving when all others are forsaking, it never fails or falters, even though the heart is breaking."
—Helen Rice

• • •

"The mother love is like God's love; he loves us not because we are lovable, but because it is His nature to love, and because we are His children."
—Earl Riney

• • •

"Don't let [it] dim your sparkle. But if it does,
I always know where to find glitter."
—KRISTINE AKINS, ENTREPRENEUR AND CREATOR OF
CHARLIECURLS, TO HER DAUGHTER, CIERA

• • •

"I admire you for the strength you've instilled in me."
—"TURN TO YOU" BY JUSTIN BIEBER,
A SONG DEDICATED TO HIS SINGLE MOM

• • •

"A mother's love is whole no matter how many times it's divided."
—ROBERT BRAULT

• • •

"You taught me everything;
Everything you've given me I'll always keep it inside;
You're the driving force in my life."
—"A SONG FOR MAMA" BY BOYZ II MEN

• • •

"All our children need is to feel love. Love them much. Love them
hard. Love them unconditionally. (And make sure they know it.)"
—CAROLINA KING, *MAMA INSTINCTS*

• • •

"I know you were on my side even when I was wrong;
And I love you for giving me your eyes,
staying back and watching me shine."
—"THE BEST DAY" BY TAYLOR SWIFT

• • •

"The instant of birth is exquisite. Pain and joy are one at this moment. Ever after, the dim recollection is so sweet that we speak to our children with a gratitude they never understand."
—MADELINE TIGER

• • •

"One generation full of deeply loving parents would change the brain of the next generation, and with that, the world."
—CHARLES RAISON

• • •

"Who doesn't know Mother Teresa, the Epitome of Compassion; by her life example, she gave hope and life by reaching out to the destitute of this world, and so today she lives not only in the heavens but in the hearts of the human race."
—DR. JEANETTE PINTO, FORMER PRINCIPAL OF SOPHIA COLLEGE AND AUTHOR OF *WONDER WOMEN OF INDIA*

• • •

"Their heart is a garden. Your words are the seeds.
You can grow flowers, or you can grow weeds."
—ZOE KIM, ON MOTHERS SPEAKING TO THEIR CHILDREN

• • •

"My mother was a life giver. Oh, I wish I had had the eyes to see
and the heart to appreciate all that she did and spent on and for
me while she was still alive."
—STASI ELDREDGE

• • •

"We're all imperfect parents and that's perfectly ok.
Tiny humans need connection not perfection."
—L. R. KNOST

• • •

"Mothering is the gospel lived out as you hold your child's heart in beauty, prayer, and patience. It's not the big decisions, but the little ones, trusting God through it all."
—ELIZABETH HAWN

• • •

"'Life-giving' is the most powerful, influential and eternal thing that you'll ever do in this life."
—NANCY CAMPBELL, *ABOVE RUBIES*

• • •

"You are My Sun, My Moon, and All My Stars."
—E. E. CUMMINGS

• • •

"A woman in birth is at once her most powerful, and most vulnerable. But any woman who has birthed unhindered understands that we are stronger than we know."
—MARCIE MACARI

• • •

"Your words as a parent have great power. Use them wisely and make sure they come from the heart."
—CAROLINA KING, *MAMA INSTINCTS*

• • •

"A mother's love liberates."
—MAYA ANGELOU

• • •

"Mothers can forgive anything! Tell me all, and be sure that I will never let you go, though the whole world should turn from you."
—LOUISA MAY ALCOTT, *Jo's Boys*

• • •

"Whatever else is unsure in this stinking dunghill of a world, a mother's love is not."
—JAMES JOYCE

• • •

"Jesus taught that providing shelter for the shelterless, food for the hungry, and clothing for the naked are sacred acts. They're also the hallmark activities of mothering. When we do them from the right motive for those in our homes, it's as if we've done them for Christ Himself."
—JEN WILKIN

• • •

"As you wander through this troubled world
In search of all things beautiful
You can close your eyes when you're miles away
And hear my voice like a serenade."
—"LULLABY" BY DIXIE CHICKS

• • •

"One must still have chaos in oneself to be able to give
birth to a dancing star."
—FRIEDRICH NIETZSCHE

• • •

"Birth isn't something we suffer, but something we
actively do and exult in."
—SHEILA KITZINGER

• • •

"[Motherhood is] a choice you make every day, to put someone else's happiness and well-being ahead of your own, to teach the hard lessons, to do the right thing even when you're not sure what the right thing is . . . and to forgive yourself, over and over again, for doing everything wrong."
—DONNA BALL, *AT HOME ON LADYBUG FARM*

• • •

"A powerful phrase your child needs to hear every day—I love you no matter what."
—CAROLINA KING, *MAMA INSTINCTS*

• • •

"Loving a child doesn't mean giving in to all his whims; to love him is to bring out the best in him, to teach him to love what is difficult."
—NADIA BOULANGER

• • •

"Women are the life givers, teachers, the keepers of
water and so much more."
—JUDITH SAYERS, FIRST NATIONS IN
BC KNOWLEDGE NETWORK

• • •

"Being a mother is like being a gardener of souls. You tend your
children, make sure the light always touches them; you nourish
them. You sow your seeds, and reap what you sow."
—KAREN WHITE, *SEA CHANGE*

• • •

"The first woman and mother was given the name 'Eve' which
means 'life.' What a bold reflection of our life-giving God!
Women have been made to be life givers."
—SHELLY SCHWALM

• • •

"The sweetest devotion
Hitting me like an explosion."
—"SWEETEST DEVOTION" BY ADELE,
A SONG SHE WROTE FOR HER DAUGHTER

• • •

"Mother is a verb. It's something you do. Not just who you are."
—CHERYL LACEY DONOVAN

• • •

"There is no greater heaven than the heart of a loving
mother. She takes care of you when you are still in her womb.
She nurtures you after you are born. She hurts when you
fall . . . She is the only person who genuinely cares about you.
She loves you as she loves herself."
—BANGAMBIKI HABYARIMANA,
THE GREAT PEARL OF WISDOM

• • •

"I'll love you forever, I'll like you for always,
as long as I'm living my baby you'll be."
—ROBERT MUNSCH, *LOVE YOU FOREVER*

• • •

"What is the secret weapon of women who have been life giving?
The answer is simple a four-letter word . . . LOVE."
—DR. JEANETTE PINTO, FORMER PRINCIPAL OF SOPHIA
COLLEGE AND AUTHOR OF *WONDER WOMEN OF INDIA*

• • •

"We are the windows through which our children first see the
world. Let us be conscious of the view."
—KATRINA KENISON, *MITTEN STRINGS FOR GOD*

• • •

"[My mother] had handed down respect for the possibilities—and the will to grasp them."
—ALICE WALKER

• • •

"While women and men were created equal, and they both were assigned the joint task of bearing children and subduing the earth, they were uniquely created different. Eve by the very meaning of her name is a 'life-giver' —she was created to bring life into the world!"
—LINDSAY EDMONDS, PASSIONATE HOMEMAKING

• • •

"Birth is the pinnacle where women discover
the courage to become mothers."
—ANITA DIAMANT

3

A Mother's Intuition

"There will always be critics so do what feels right to you."
—CAROLINA KING, *MAMA INSTINCTS*

• • •

"They say 'don't mess with mama bears' and 'a mother's intuition
is always right' and it's entirely true—do whatever you can
to affirm and further connect with your powerful God-given
intuition; it's the best tool to guide you no matter what others are
saying during difficult or complex decisions."
—AMBER SIMS HINTERPLATTNER, MOTHER, HEALTH-CHOICE
ADVOCATE, AND AWARD-WINNING ENTREPRENEUR

• • •

"The mother is almost always right.
A mother's intuition is paramount."
—DR. DANIEL R. TAYLOR

• • •

"Don't stand unmoving outside the door of a crying baby whose only desire is to touch you. Go to your baby. Go to your baby a million times. Demonstrate that people can be trusted, that the environment can be trusted, that we live in a benign universe."
—PEGGY O'MARA, AUTHOR OF *NATURAL FAMILY LIVING*

• • •

"I feel there are two people inside me—me and my intuition.
If I go against her, she'll screw me every time,
and if I follow her, we get along quite nicely."
—KIM BASINGER

• • •

"A wise mother knows: It is her state of consciousness that
matters. Her gentleness and clarity command respect.
Her love creates security."
—VIMALA MCCLURE, *THE TAO OF MOTHERHOOD*

• • •

"She will even give upon herself and her dreams,
but not on you and your dreams."
—LUFFINA LOURDURAJ

• • •

"Follow your instincts: If something smells bad, tastes bad, or
in any way has you questioning if it is safe—don't give it to your
kids. When I smelled the lead paint fumes at our house I grabbed
the kids and took them away, but I didn't do it quickly enough
and they were poisoned."
—TAMARA RUBIN, LEAD SAFE MAMA, AWARD-WINNING
ENVIRONMENTAL ACTIVIST AND DOCUMENTARY FILMMAKER
AND MOTHER OF LEAD-POISONED KIDS

• • •

"Many of our problems in US maternity care stem from the fact that we leave no room for recognizing when nature is smarter than we are."
—INA MAY GASKIN, *BIRTH MATTERS: A MIDWIFE'S MANIFESTA*

• • •

"A child's hand in yours —what tenderness and power it arouses. You are instantly the very touchstone of wisdom and strength."
—MARJORIE HOLMES

• • •

"Most mothers are instinctive philosophers."
—HARRIET BEECHER STOWE

• • •

"Once you're a mom, you're always a mom.
It's like riding a bike, you never forget."
—Taraji P. Henson

• • •

"As women we are born to mother. By nature we are intended to grow something from nothing into a blossoming soul. However we go about it does not matter; it is instinctual."
—Megan Gilger, *The Fresh Exchange*

• • •

"You will see things. Feel things. Know things. Those that are trying to hide it, will deny it. Trust your gut. You know the truth."
—YOGA PROVERB

• • •

"The easiest way to get your children to listen to you and to learn from you, is by connecting with them first."
—CAROLINA KING, *MAMA INSTINCTS*

• • •

"You are your baby's best expert."
—DR. WILLIAM SEARS, *THE BABY BOOK*

• • •

"Who can justly measure the righteous influence of a mother's love? What enduring fruits result from the seeds of truth that a mother carefully plants and lovingly cultivates in the fertile soil of a child's trusting mind and heart? As a mother, you have been given divine instincts to help you sense your child's special talents and unique capacities."
—RICHARD G. SCOTT

● ● ●

"A mother understands what a child does not say."
—JEWISH PROVERB

● ● ●

"Trust yourself. You know more than you think you do."
—DR. BENJAMIN SPOCK

● ● ●

"I was in the ecstasy of babies then. I was on a long, oxytocin high. No one told me about this. No one told me I would feel like a wild animal ready to kill or be killed at a moment's notice with no hesitation at all right now for my baby."
—PEGGY O'MARA, PUBLISHER OF *MOTHERING MAGAZINE*

• • •

"When you are a mother, you are never really alone in your thoughts. A mother always has to think twice, once for herself and once for her child."
—SOPHIA LOREN

• • •

"Every mama knows what's best for her child, if she truly listens to what her heart is saying."
—CAROLINA KING, *MAMA INSTINCTS*

• • •

"I know how to do anything—I'm a mom."
—Roseanne Barr

• • •

"It is not until you become a mother that your judgment
slowly turns to compassion and understanding."
—Erma Bombeck

• • •

"Intuition becomes increasingly valuable in the new
information society precisely because there is so much data."
—John Naisbitt

• • •

"Motherhood is full of seasons and as many of the seasoned moms said, 'This too shall pass.'"
—JENNIFER ROSKAMP, *A REALISTIC ACTION PLAN FOR THE WEARY MOM*

• • •

"Intuition is a spiritual faculty and does not explain, but simply points the way."
—FLORENCE SCOVEL SHINN

• • •

"Good instincts usually tell you what to do long before your head has figured it out."
—MICHAEL BURKE

• • •

"I can truly say how wonderful I feel my mother is. She knows exactly when I'm in need, not to mention all the things she does."
—JULIE HEBERT

• • •

"Intuition is more than knowledge, and truth comes pure from the heart."
—DON BRADLEY

• • •

"There is a religion in all deep love, but the love of a mother is the veil of a softer light between the heart and the heavenly Father."
—SAMUEL TAYLOR COLERIDGE

• • •

"Trust your hunches. They're usually based on facts filed away just below the conscious level."
—DR. JOYCE BROTHERS

• • •

"Trust your own instinct. Your mistakes might as well be your own, instead of someone else's."
—BILLY WILDER

• • •

"Follow your instincts. That's where true wisdom manifests itself."
—OPRAH WINFREY

• • •

"You are the perfect mama for your child. Never forget that."
—CAROLINA KING, *MAMA INSTINCTS*

• • •

"The fastest way to break the cycle of perfectionism and become a fearless mother is to give up the idea of doing it perfectly—indeed to embrace uncertainty and imperfection."
—ARIANNA HUFFINGTON

• • •

"Intuition is a spiritual faculty and does not explain, but simply points the way."
—FLORENCE SCOVEL SHINN

• • •

"Your inner knowing is your only true compass."
—JOY PAGE

• • •

"Listen to your inner voice . . . for it is a deep and powerful
source of wisdom, beauty, and truth, ever flowing through you."
—CAROLINE JOY ADAMS

4

Realities of Modern-Day Motherhood

"Is my house perfectly clean? No. But am I doing my very best to keep things tidy? Also no."
—ELISE NEW, *THE FRUGAL FARM WIFE*

• • •

"If some YouTube star could create a 'Clean Your Room Challenge' or even a 'Put Your Clothes in the Hamper Challenge,' that would be awesome.
—JESSICA WATSON, *FOUR PLUS AN ANGEL*

• • •

"I'm a mom and a psychologist. In other words, I am acutely
aware of all the things I am doing wrong."
—@MOMPSYCHOLOGIST

• • •

"I don't know who needs to hear this right now, but your worth as
a partner and mother is not defined by how clean your house is."
—CHRISTIE KLEIN, MOTHER AND SMALL BUSINESS OWNER AT
SEW WHAT BY CK

• • •

"Breastfeeding helps you unwind from a busy day's work and
reconnect with your baby, especially after a tense day."
—DR. WILLIAM SEARS, THE ATTACHMENT PARENTING BOOK

• • •

"I would say to any single parent currently feeling the weight of stereotype or stigmatization that I am prouder of my years as a single mother than of any other part of my life."
—J. K. ROWLING

• • •

"Next time someone questions your parenting style, ignore them and move on. No one knows your child better than you do and when you listen to your heart you will always do what's best for your child."
—CAROLINA KING, *MAMA INSTINCTS*

• • •

"I've learned that you cannot judge the way another person is raising their kid. Everybody is just doing the best they can. It's hard to be a mom."
—MAGGIE GYLLENHAAL

• • •

"Women gain social influence through their roles as mothers, transmitters of culture, and parents for the next generation."
—PATRICIA HILL COLLINS

• • •

"My kid can't remember if he brushed his teeth this morning, but he can remember that last Wednesday at 4:07 p.m. it was cloudy and we were at the grocery store and he was wearing his Star Wars shirt and we were in Aisle 7 and I muttered that 'maybe next time' I would buy him that ice cream."
—LESLIE MEANS, *HER VIEW FROM HOME*

• • •

"My home is green enough to be healthy but chill enough to be happy."
—LEAH SEGEDIE, *GREEN ENOUGH*

• • •

"I really think people need to be a little more supportive and a little less critical of mothers, especially in stores . . . It's OK to not want to read the same book again tonight. It's OK to lock yourself in your room and binge watch *The Great British Baking Show*. It's OK to run out after the grocery store and leave your kids with your husband because you need an hour of alone time at the nail salon . . . What's not OK is to judge another mother or say something to her that isn't helpful—when she's clearly at the end of her rope."
—KRISTEN HEWITT

• • •

"One of the hardest parts of parenting is trying to keep a straight face when your kid does something naughty but hilarious. It's like, 'as a human, I find this thing that you did very funny.' But as a mother this isn't ok."
—CARISSA BONHAM, *CREATIVE GREEN LIVING*

• • •

"Being a mom has made me so tired. And so happy."
—TINA FEY

• • •

"[Tracy Loeppky] began as we all do, as a mother. A working mother not quite knowing what life had in store for her, but she was in it for the long haul and willing to go where her heart led her."
—*BIRTH OF A WOMAN* MAGAZINE

• • •

"Even in the cartoon world, Wonder Woman in all her glory never raised children, stabilized a husband, or cleaned and managed a house. Wonder Woman faced only criminals, not housework horrors."
—DON ASLET, *IS THERE LIFE AFTER HOUSEWORK?*

• • •

"The phrase 'working mother' is redundant."
—JANE SELLMAN

• • •

"Unless we are willing to encourage our children to reconnect with and appreciate the natural world, we can't expect them to help protect and care for it."
—DAVID SUZUKI

• • •

"To have a child is an irrevocable shift of lifestyle. It is a transition of priorities, routines, and day-to-day goals. Where once I might have called a day a "success" if I cleared out the starred folder of my work inbox, for example, I now call a day a "success" if neither of my children poops through their outfit."
—MARIE SOUTHARD OSPINA, "HOW IMPORTANT IS IT THAT YOU MAKE FRIENDS WITH OTHER MOMS?" FOR ROMPER

• • •

"I'd get a lot more sleep if I didn't insist on reading the entire Internet every night before bed."
—ADRIANNE SURIAN

• • •

"At work, you think of the children you have left at home. At home, you think of the work you've left unfinished. Such a struggle is unleashed within yourself."
—GOLDA MEIR

• • •

"If you like a toddler staring you square in the vagina as you change your tampon, then motherhood is right up your alley."
—RACHEL SOBEL, *WHINE AND CHEEZ (ITS)*

• • •

"I don't think you necessarily have to be part of a traditional nuclear family to be a good mother."
—MARY LOUISE PARKER

• • •

"Treat your children like whole humans from the moment they are born. Your use of clear language and honesty from the beginning in all things (including around topics like Santa and the Easter Bunny) will shape who they become and what they prioritize in their lives. Never lie to your children."
—TAMARA RUBIN, LEAD SAFE MAMA, AWARD WINNING ENVIRONMENTAL ACTIVIST AND DOCUMENTARY FILMMAKER

• • •

"You will never realize your full potential for speed and agility until the day you see your toddler holding a Sharpie marker."
—@THEBABYLADY7

• • •

"By and large, mothers and housewives are the only workers who do not have regular time off. They are the great vacationless class."
—ANNE MORROW LINDBERGH

• • •

"If evolution really works, how come mothers only have two hands?"
—MILTON BERLE

• • •

"Any other parents out there go into panic mode when presented with an hour of alone time?
Should I read a book?
Clean the house?
Take up knitting?
Learn German?
Train for my black belt?
Solve world hunger?
OMG, do all the things!!!
Andddd your hour is up."
—BECCA CARNAHAN @WITH_LOVE_BECCA

• • •

"I think moms, single or not, put a lot of pressure on ourselves trying to balance it all. It's NEVER going to be perfectly balanced—the sooner you know this, the sooner you can relieve some of the pressure you put on yourself."
—DENISE RICHARDS

• • •

"A Modern Mom to me is not always someone that juggles a career and family. A Modern Mom is a woman who takes care of herself on the inside and the outside."
—REGINA KING

• • •

"So it turns out that as an adult you can eat chocolate cake for breakfast if you want . . . there is literally no one policing this!"
—REBECCA COOPER, *SIMPLE AS THAT* BLOG

• • •

"Motherhood is not for the faint-hearted. Frogs, skinned knees, and the insults of teenage girls are not meant for the wimpy."
—DANIELLE STEEL

• • •

"It's a little scary sometimes. I'm always thinking, like, am I teaching her a bad habit by doing this? So it's a lot of worry in that we're shaping her whole personality, her future, how she thinks about the world. And that's kind of stressful. It's a little bit of pressure. But it's good. I like it. It's been fun."
—KASEY NORBERG, *MATERNAL INSTINCT*

• • •

"Motherhood has a very humanizing effect.
Everything gets reduced to essentials."
—MERYL STREEP

• • •

"I think every working mom probably feels the same thing: You go through big chunks of time where you're just thinking, 'This is impossible—oh, this is impossible.' And then you just keep going and keep going, and you sort of do the impossible."
—TINA FEY

• • •

"Some days I make beautiful dinners from scratch. Today my kids had cereal and ice cream for dinner. At least it was organic."
—CARISSA BONHAM

• • •

"When it comes to parenting, the practice of framing mothers and fathers as good or bad is both rampant and corrosive—it turns parenting into a shame minefield. The real questions for parents should be: 'Are you engaged? Are you paying attention?'
—BRENÉ BROWN, *DARING GREATLY*

• • •

"Six-pack abs are great! But my body literally rearranged its organs to bring another life into the world, so maybe my stomach is pretty damn impressive, too."
—@SALTYMERMAIDENT

• • •

"I saw a quote that said 'Your kids don't need a perfect mom. They need a happy one.' And I thought more moms should see it."
—BARBARA MCKELL, *REIKI KIDS* (REIKIKIDS.CA)

• • •

"If baby is thriving, but Mom is completely burned out because she is not getting the help she needs, something has to change."
—DR. WILLIAM SEARS

• • •

"Mothering Oxymoron: Reminding the kids to not talk with food in their mouths, yet I have food in my mouth while trying to correct them in the moment."
—DEBBIE BARBUTO, A.K.A. MOMMY MOO MOO

• • •

"Every family is different. I am mom and I am dad and I'm going to do my best. You should be proud, walk through life saying I have the coolest family. I am part of a modern family."
—RICKY MARTIN

• • •

"Now, mothering is far more rewarding than any job, but there are times when you need a day off."
—ASHLEE MEADOWS, *STRESS MANAGEMENT*

• • •

"FIRST RULE OF PARENT CLUB: You don't talk about activities in front of the kids unless you are fully prepared to engage in said activities."
—@MOMPSYCHOLOGIST

• • •

"Unless your parenting advice is which wine pairs best with 3 weeks of laundry, keep it to yourself."
—ALLY PROBST, COAUTHOR OF *THE DAD BOOK*

• • •

"Giving grace to yourself is never more important than
when you become a mother."
—WHITNEY MEADE, *THE BALANCE BEAM*

• • •

"Motherhood has relaxed me in many ways. You learn to
deal with crisis. I've become a juggler, I suppose. It's all a big
circus, and nobody who knows me believes I can manage,
but sometimes I do."
—JANE SEYMOUR

• • •

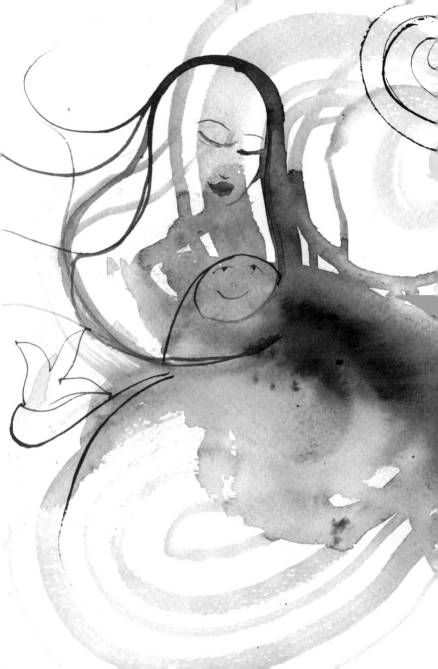

5

As Fierce as a Mama Bear

"I am a mother. There is no braver work than that."
—Robyn O'Brien, activist and author of *The Unhealthy Truth*

• • •

"Becoming a mom gave me greater courage to stand up for what I believe in. It's a big role that I didn't fully understand until I actually became a mother. Convictions are crystalized and protecting your child becomes the single most important priority in a world where profits are often prioritized over people."
—Amber Sims Hinterplattner, mother, health-choice advocate, and award-winning entrepreneur

• • •

"There's absolutely nothing a mother wouldn't do for her children. There's no length too great, no river too wide, and NO mountain too high. Mothers are the skeletal structure of our society; the bond created between mother and child can never be severed."
—BREEAUNA SAGDAL, FAMILY RIGHTS ADVOCATE AND PACNW REGIONAL DIRECTOR FOR PUNISHED4PROTECTING

• • •

"These arms don't get tired. They carry babies."
—OVERHEARD AT THE CALIFORNIA ASSEMBLY APPROPRIATIONS SUSPENSE FILE HEARING ON AUGUST 30, 2019 WHEN TARA THORNTON, DENISE AGUILAR, AND HEIDI MUNOZ GLEISNER STOOD ON CHAIRS TO PROTEST SB276

• • •

"Remember that a single mom is just like any other mom and that our number one priority is to our kids. Any parent does whatever it takes for their kids and a single mother is no different."
—PAULA MIRANDA

• • •

"If we could allow Mama Bear to show her teeth not just when our own child is hurting but when we see another human being suffer, I am convinced that we as mothers, could wreak havoc on injustice and summon radical, forceful, lumbering change. We could be the protectors of not just our own offspring, but of the baby bears all over the world."
—Leslie Klipsch, *Mama Bear's Manifesto*

• • •

"Not only am I a fighter, but I'm a survivor. I think being a mother really plays into that."
—Willow Cross, *Getting Over It*

• • •

"Stop asking how good you are and start asking
what the world needs."
— UNKNOWN (SHARED BY CAROLINA KING,
MAMA INSTINCTS)

• • •

"Every mom has a mission to love, guide, and protect her family.
Don't mess with her while she's on it."
—VICKI REECE

• • •

"I hadn't realized how suppressed this ferocious Goddess energy
had been in me. Everything in my childhood upbringing, in
my Christian church conditioning, in my medical education—
reinforced how I'm supposed to just push down anger, suppress
outrage, suck it up in the face of injustice, and tolerate abuses
of power. Going through this trauma awakened something in
me that had been long dormant, and for this activation, I am
grateful, even in the midst of the pain of what I experienced."
—LISSA RANKIN

• • •

"Sometimes the strength of motherhood is greater
than natural laws."
—Barbara Kingsolver

• • •

"I was still numb from my child's unexpected diagnosis when
a small voice inside me wondered what we were going to
do. Then my mama bear voice answered back loud and clear
'whatever it takes'—and that's why you never mess with a
special needs mother."
—Kiera Young

• • •

"To describe my mother would be to write about a hurricane in
its perfect power. Or the climbing, falling colors of a rainbow."
—Maya Angelou

• • •

"Why should a woman's right to choose extend to her reproductive organs but not her (or her children's) immune systems?"
—STEPHEN SLOAN OF THE HUMAN LEADERSHIP CONFERENCE (IN A LETTER WRITTEN TO OREGON LAWMAKERS)

• • •

"There is no greater warrior than a mother protecting her child."
—N. K. JEMISIN

• • •

"My time in pharma taught me that just because something is on the market doesn't mean it's safe."
—BRANDY VAUGHAN, FORMER MERCK SALES EXECUTIVE AND LEARN THE RISK FOUNDER

• • •

"Mothers and their children are in a category all their own.
There's no bond so strong in the entire world."
—Gail Tsukiyama

• • •

"Because when it comes to my offspring I will fight with the fangs
of a wolf and the claws of a dragon. And no one, or nothing will
stop me from protecting them."
—Jordan Sarah Weatherhead

• • •

"A good mama bear knows when to growl and when to grin."
—Nancy Jergins, imom.com

• • •

"I couldn't keep quiet. We needed everyone to know, even if nobody believed us. That's probably why they called us the Mad Mothers at first."
—HAYDÉE GASTELÚ, ONE OF THE MOTHERS OF PLAZA DE MAYO, ON HER EXPERIENCE PROTESTING THE KIDNAPPING OF ARGENTINIAN CHILDREN IN THE 1970S

• • •

"Being a working mother and a working single parent instills in you a sense of determination."
—FELICITY JONES

• • •

"Motherhood has completely changed me. It's just about like the most completely humbling experience that I've ever had. I think that it puts you in your place because it really forces you to address the issues that you claim to believe in, and if you can't stand up to those principles when you're raising a child, forget it."
—DIANE KEATON

• • •

"There's no bitch on earth like a mother frightened for her kids."
—STEPHEN KING

• • •

"Yes, Greta Thunberg is one person: a fierce, glorious, beautiful person. You are one person too, equally fierce and glorious and beautiful. That's enough to make history. You just have to move."
—JOHN PAVLOVITZ, AUTHOR OF *A BIGGER TABLE*

• • •

"The only thing standing between a child and industry corruption is a mom."
—ROBERT F. KENNEDY JR., CHILDREN'S HEALTH DEFENSE

• • •

"There are three types of people:
Those who stand beside the ring and cheer.
Those who stand beside the ring and complain.
And those who step into the ring and right for the
health of our families and future."
—ROBYN O'BRIEN, ACTIVIST AND AUTHOR OF *THE
UNHEALTHY TRUTH*

• • •

"I love my children more than they love their money."
—SANDRA EFRAIMSON, RN, CALENDULA HEALING (AS SHE
WAS BEING ARRESTED FOR PEACEFULLY PROTESTING SB276,
A BILL WHICH WOULD BAN KIDS IN CALIFORNIA FROM
ATTENDING SCHOOL IF THEY HAD MEDICAL REASONS TO
AVOID ONE OR MORE REQUIRED VACCINES)

• • •

"People will try to get you off course, some will seduce you into taking yourself off that course and others will make it their mission to torpedo you and sink you, others will tell you they know the best course for you and demand or convince you to instead follow them. . . . Never relent. In being unrelenting you will attract others who are on the same course, and you as an individual ship become one of many, a united fleet for freedom."
—Jonathan Lockwood, Conscience Coalition

● ● ●

"A mother's love for her child is like nothing else in the world. It knows no law, no pity. It dares all things and crushes down remorselessly all that stands in its path."
—Agatha Christie, "The Last Séance" from *The Hound of Death and Other Stories*

● ● ●

"We so often think of our mothers that way—as great protectors, our last line of defense when, no matter the enemy or the age, we are at our most vulnerable"
—BRUCE LOWRY, *NORTH JERSEY RECORD* (ON HIS MOTHER NURTURING HIM BACK TO HEALTH AT AGE THREE)

• • •

"There is no friendship, no love, like that of a mother for her child."
—HENRY WARD BEECHER

• • •

"Creating a corporate bureaucracy, and a culture of fear, which is placed between parental rights, is the fastest way to degrade future generations, and our society as a whole. When parents are forced to make fear-based decisions, rather than what's best for their child, parents lose their ability to effectively parent."
—Breeauna Sagdal, family rights advocate and PACNW regional director for Punished4Protecting

• • •

"Being a mother is learning about strengths you didn't know you had, and dealing with fears you didn't know existed."
—Linda Wooten

• • •

6

There's Nobody Like Mom

"I realized when you look at your mother, you are looking at the purest love you will ever know."
—MITCH ALBOM

• • •

"There is ONE soul above all others—
That you must always show patience, respect, and trust
And this woman is your mother."
—SUZY KASSEM, *RISE UP AND SALUTE THE SUN:
THE WRITINGS OF SUZY KASSEM*

• • •

"Mother was anchor. Mother was comfort. Mother was home. A girl who lost her mother was suddenly a tiny boat on an angry ocean. Some boats eventually floated ashore. And some boats, like me, seemed to float farther and farther from land."
—RUTA SEPETYS, *SALT TO THE SEA*

• • •

"She sacrifices her dreams to make my dream come true."
—LUFFINA LOURDURAJ

• • •

"The best place to cry is on a mother's arms."
—JODI PICOULT

• • •

"A mother is the truest friend we have, when trials heavy and sudden fall upon us; when adversity takes the place of prosperity; when friends desert us; when trouble thickens around us, still will she cling to us, and endeavor by her kind precepts and counsels to dissipate the clouds of darkness, and cause peace to return to our hearts."
—WASHINGTON IRVING

• • •

"A mother's arms are more comforting than anyone else's."
—PRINCESS DIANA

• • •

"Mother —that was the bank where we deposited all our hurts and worries."
—T. DEWITT TALMAGE

• • •

"Dear mama, don't you know I love you?
Dear mama, place no one above you"
—"DEAR MAMA" BY TUPAC

• • •

"I cannot forget my mother. She is my bridge.
When I needed to get across, she steadied herself long
enough for me to run across safely."
—RENITA WEEMS

• • •

"She is a woman of strength and dignity and has no fear of
old age. When she speaks, her words are wise, and kindness
is the rule for everything she says. She watches carefully all
that goes on throughout her household and is never lazy. Her
children stand and bless her; so does her husband. He praises
her with these words: 'There are many fine women in the world,
but you are the best of them all!'"
—PROVERBS 31:25-29 LIVING BIBLE (TLB)

• • •

"The moment he wakes up from a nap. . . . Just a gummy mouth, no teeth, just a big smile, happy that you're alive and you're just looking at him. That's probably the most magical."
—JESSICA BIEL

● ● ●

"A mother is one to whom you hurry when you are troubled."
— EMILY DICKINSON

● ● ●

"You showed me when I was young just how to grow;
You showed me everything that I should know;
You showed me, just how to walk without your hands;
'Cause mom you always were the perfect fan."
—"THE PERFECT FAN" BY BACKSTREET BOYS

● ● ●

"My mother is my root, my foundation. She planted the seed that I base my life on, and that is the belief that the ability to achieve starts in your mind."
—MICHAEL JORDAN

• • •

"A mother is a woman who shows you the light when you just see the dark."
—GRIMALDOS ROBIN

• • •

"Roses are red
violets are blue
There is no one dearer
than a Mom like you!"
—KATE SUMMERS

• • •

"*Mother*: the most beautiful word on the lips of mankind."
—KAHLIL GIBRAN

• • •

"My mother was the dearest, sweetest angel. She didn't talk;
she sang. She was a tower of strength."
—JAYNE MEADOWS

• • •

"There ought to be a hall of fame for mamas, creation's most
unique and precious pearl, and heaven help us always to
remember, that the hand that rocks the cradle rules the world."
— GLEN CAMPBELL

• • •

"So, mother, I thank you, for all you've done and still do;
You got me, I got you, together we always pull through."
—"OH MOTHER" BY CHRISTINA AGUILERA

• • •

"Mother was by far the greatest personal influence in our lives."
—DWIGHT EISENHOWER

• • •

"I have a special mother, this I truly know.
I could not ask for better, my mother, I love her so."
—JULIE HUBERT

• • •

"Whenever I thought about my mother, I envisioned an angel."
—LUDVIK WIEDER, *I PROMISED MY MOTHER*

• • •

"If every mother in the United States could wrap her
mind around her true value as a woman and mother,
her life would never be the same."
—MEG MEEKER MD, *THE 10 HABITS OF HAPPY MOTHERS*

• • •

"You might have a mom, she might be the bomb,
but ain't nobody got a mom like mine."
—"MOM" BY MEGHAN TRAINOR

• • •

"A mother's arms are made of tenderness, and children sleep
soundly in them."
—VICTOR HUGO

• • •

"I love my mother as the trees love water and sunshine;
she helps me grow, prosper, and reach great heights."
—TERRI GUILLEMETS

• • •

"God could not be everywhere, and therefore he made mothers."
—RUDYARD KIPLING

• • •

"My mom is a hard worker. She puts her head down and she gets it done. And she finds a way to have fun. She always says, 'Happiness is your own responsibility.' That's probably what I quote from her and live by the most."
—JENNIFER GARNER

• • •

"Our mothers always remain the strangest, craziest people we've ever met."
—MARGUERITE DURAS

• • •

"[My mother] was invaluable to me—the most influential person in my life."
—STEVE HARVEY, *ACT LIKE A LADY, THINK LIKE A MAN*

• • •

"Mama was my greatest teacher, a teacher of compassion, love and fearlessness. If love is sweet as a flower, then my mother is that sweet flower of love."
—STEVIE WONDER

• • •

"There is no role in life more essential and more eternal than that of motherhood."
—M. RUSSELL BALLARD

• • •

"Most of all the other beautiful things in life come by twos and threes by dozens and hundreds. Plenty of roses, stars, sunsets, rainbows, brothers, and sisters, aunts and cousins, but only one mother in the whole world."
—KATE DOUGLAS WIGGIN

• • •

"Ain't a woman alive that can take my momma's place."
—"DEAR MAMA" BY TUPAC

• • •

"My mother was the most beautiful woman I ever saw. All I am I owe to my mother. I attribute all my success in life to the moral, intellectual, and physical education I received from her."
—GEORGE WASHINGTON

• • •

"Mothers hold their children's hands for a short while, but their hearts forever."
—NITYA PRAKASH

• • •

"A mother is she who can take the place of all others but whose place no one else can take."
—CARDINAL MERMILLOD

• • •

"Mothers are the deities worth worshipping for the rest of our lives."
—LOIS KASHAM ASHIM

• • •

"I believe in love at first sight, because I've been loving my mother since I opened my eyes."
—INDIAN PROVERB

• • •

"There will be so many times you feel like you've failed, but in the eyes, heart, and mind of your child, you are super mom."
—STEPHANIE PRECOURT

• • •

"My mother taught me about the power of inspiration and courage, and she did it with a strength and a passion that I wish could be bottled."
—CARLY FIORINA

• • •

"My mother is a poem I'll never be able to write, though everything I write is a poem to my mother."
—SHARON DOUBIAGO

• • •

"For the mother is and must be, whether she knows it or not, the greatest, strongest, and most lasting teacher her children have."
—HANNAH W. SMITH

• • •

"My mom is my hero. She inspired me to dream when I was a kid, so anytime anyone inspires you to dream, that's gotta be your hero."
—TIM MCGRAW

• • •

"My mother . . . she is beautiful, softened at the edges and tempered with a spine of steel. I want to grow old and be like her."
—JODI PICOULT

• • •

"All that I am or ever hope to be, I owe to my angel mother."
—ABRAHAM LINCOLN

• • •

"Mothers connect us all to the sacred."
—NATIVE HOPE

• • •

7

For the Mothers of Differently Wired Kids

"Until you have a kid with special needs you have no idea of the depth of your strength, tenacity, and resourcefulness."
—Unknown

• • •

"By loving them for more than their abilities we show our children that they are much more than the sum of their accomplishments."
—Eileen Kennedy-Moore, *Smart Parenting for Smart Kids*

• • •

"I'd choose you in a hundred lifetimes; in a hundred worlds, in any version of reality, I'd find you and I'd choose you."
—KIERSTEN WHITE

• • •

"There's no way to be a perfect mother and a million ways to be a good one."
—JILL CHURCHILL

• • •

"We teach our children courage simply by showing up as we are, trusting our voices, and advocating for what we and those we love need. Don't be afraid to stand in your power."
—BRITTANY SCHIAVONE, BRITTANY'S BASKETS OF HOPE

• • •

"Me at the IEP meeting: 'I just took a DNA test.
Turns out, I'm 100% THAT MOM.'"
—Phoebe Holmes

• • •

"It shouldn't matter how slowly a child learns. What matters is
that we encourage them to never stop trying."
—Robert John Meehan

• • •

"Parents of children with special needs create their own world of
happiness and believe in things that others cannot yet see."
—Unknown

• • •

"I dwell in possibility."
—EMILY DICKINSON

• • •

"Motherhood is about raising and celebrating the child you have, not the child you thought you would have. It's about understanding that he is exactly the person he is supposed to be and that, if you're lucky, he just might be the teacher who turns you into the person you are supposed to be."
—JOAN RYAN

• • •

"We have no special needs children. Just children . . . with special needs."
—UWE MAURER

• • •

"Courage does not always roar. Sometimes courage is the quiet voice at the end of the day saying, 'I will try again tomorrow.'"
—MARY ANNE RADMACHE

• • •

"We are more alike, my friends, than we are unalike."
—MAYA ANGELOU

• • •

"To be nobody but yourself in a world which is doing its best, night and day, to make you everybody else—means to fight the hardest battle which any human being can fight; never stop fighting."
—E. E. CUMMINGS

• • •

"Some of the most wonderful people are the ones who
don't fit into boxes."
—TORI AMOS

• • •

"My son Avi has a brain injury from being lead poisoned as
a baby. I was told by so many, 'Don't let him know he is lead
poisoned, because he will feel *less than*.' I ignored that advice
from day one. We let him know WHY he has the challenges he
has—and that he is not defined by his challenges any more than
someone with a broken leg is defined by their inability to walk
without crutches. We worked with his strengths to give him every
opportunity to succeed. This resulted in Avi being empowered to
ask for what he needs to be and do his best."
—TAMARA RUBIN, LEAD SAFE MAMA, AWARD-WINNING
ENVIRONMENTAL ACTIVIST AND DOCUMENTARY FILMMAKER
AND MOTHER OF LEAD-POISONED KIDS

• • •

"Why fit in when you were born to stand out?"
—DR. SEUSS

• • •

"Every one of us is like the pieces of a puzzle. Each one unique and with our own special place where only we can fit, and without every one of us, the picture wouldn't be complete."
—GINA MCMURCHY-BARBER, *THE JIGSAW PUZZLE KING*

• • •

"One good mother is worth a hundred schoolmasters."
—GEORGE HERBERT

• • •

"We as a society need the millions of neurodiverse children in the world today, with their powerful gifts, talents, and abilities, to flourish. Because they are the future."
—DEBORAH REBER, *DIFFERENTLY WIRED*

• • •

"You don't know how strong you are until being strong is the only choice you have."
—BOB MARLEY

• • •

"Truly I dreamt that my beautiful mom told others my secret about life. Nicely the secret was very easy to say but harder to do. The secret is: believe in your child and believe in yourself."
—JEREMY SICILE-KIRA

• • •

"Somewhere along the line we stopped trying to fix the child that we had expected and started to enjoy the child that was."
—Meg Blomfield

• • •

"One of the secrets in life is to make stepping stones out of stumbling blocks."
—Jack Penn

• • •

"What makes a child gifted and talented may not always be good grades in school, but a different way of looking at the world and learning."
—Chuck Grassley

• • •

"No matter who you are or how you're born, you have purpose and worth. It's time we celebrate everyone's gifts and let the world know that we are stronger together!"
—BRITTANY SCHIAVONE, BRITTANY'S BASKETS OF HOPE

• • •

"It is time for parents to teach young people early on that in diversity there is beauty and there is strength."
—MAYA ANGELOU

• • •

"If you're going through hell, keep going."
—WINSTON CHURCHILL

• • •

"By holding the highest vision for your child when they cannot see it for themselves, you are lifting them up, elevating them, and helping them to soar."
—Megan Koufos

• • •

"Within every child is a connection to one form or another and a potential waiting to be fulfilled."
—Dr. Stephen Mark Shore

• • •

"Tricky. The usual parenting approaches simply don't work for us. Every decision about our child involves just a little more consideration, stress, and anxiety than what other parents might experience. It's no cakewalk."
—Deborah Reber, *Differently Wired*

• • •

"When a family focuses on ability instead of disability, all things are possible. . . . Love and acceptance is key."
—AMANDA RAE ROSS

• • •

"Without deviation from the norm, progress is not possible."
—FRANK ZAPPA

• • •

"Showing kindness towards those who are different and embracing our imperfections as proof of our humanness is the remedy for fear."
—EMMA ZURCHER-LONG

• • •

"Stop thinking about normal. . . . You don't have a big enough imagination for what your child can become."
—Johnny Seitz, in the movie *Loving Lamposts*

• • •

"Often people ask, 'How can you say you're blessed to have a son with Down syndrome?' My outlook on life has forever changed. I see my own challenges differently. He's always showing me that life is so much bigger than self."
—Yvonne Pierre, *The Day My Soul Cried: A Memoir*

• • •

"Even for parents of children who are not on the spectrum, there is no such thing as a normal child."
—Violet Stevens

• • •

"We need to embrace those who are different and the bullies need to be the ones who get off the bus."
—Caren Zucker, coauthor of *In a Different Key*

• • •

"Remember, always, that you are enough. You are exactly the parent you need to be, the one whose destiny matched perfectly with your child's. Be patient with yourself. Be compassionate. In fact, it's when you're trying your hardest and you've gone all in but you're face down on the floor that you most deserve your own compassion."
—Brittany Schiavone, Brittany's Baskets of Hope

• • •

8

On Mothering Older Children and Adults

"What she did have, after raising two children, was the equivalent of a PhD in mothering and my undying respect."
—BARBARA DELINSKY, *ESCAPE*

• • •

"Being the parent of adult kids is not easy! I've always said, "Little kids, little problems, big kids, big problems" and I didn't fully appreciate how big those problems could get when a child grew up and had adult problems."
—KAT CARPITA

• • •

"I will protect you until you are grown and then I will let you fly free, but loving you, that is for always."
—CHARLOTTE GRAY

• • •

"Please don't judge me too much until you are older and know more things."
—ANN BRASHARES, *3 WILLOWS: THE SISTERHOOD GROWS*

• • •

"Raising your child well is hard. But learning to let them go out into the world and prove that you did your job right is even tougher."
—J. CRAINE

• • •

"Call your mother. Tell her you love her. Remember,
you're the only person who knows what her heart sounds
like from the inside."
—Rachel Wolchin

• • •

"It's not what you do for your children but what you have
taught them to do for themselves that will make them
successful human beings."
—Ann Landers

• • •

"No matter how old a mother is, she watches her middle-aged
children for signs of improvement."
—Florida Scott-Maxwell

• • •

"More than one teen I know has counted on her mom to forbid something so she doesn't look to her friends like she is wimping out of something dangerous. More than one teen has begrudgingly admitted that her mom's rules were what kept her out of more trouble."
—MARIE HARTWELL-WALKER, ED.D.

• • •

"You have nothing in this world more precious than your children. When you grow old, when your hair turns white and your body grows weary, when you are prone to sit in a rocker and meditate on the things of your life, nothing will be so important as the question of how your children have turned out. . . . Do not trade your birthright as a mother for some bauble of passing value. . . . The baby you hold in your arms will grow quickly as the sunrise and sunset of the rushing days."
—GORDON B. HINCKLEY

• • •

"Why do grandparents and grandchildren get along so well?
They have the same enemy—the mother."
—CLAUDETTE COLBERT

• • •

"Grown don't mean nothing to a mother. A child is a child.
They get bigger, older, but grown? What's that supposed to mean?
In my heart it don't mean a thing."
—TONI MORRISON

• • •

"Raising children is a spur-of-the-moment, seat-of-the-
pants sort of deal, as any parent knows, particularly after an
adult child says that his most searing memory consists of
an offhand comment in the car on the way to second grade
that the parent cannot even dimly recall."
—ANNA QUINDLEN

• • •

"A mother never realizes that her children are
no longer children."
—JAMES AGEE

• • •

"There's simply no way you can tell a woman you work with that
you disapprove of her relationship with her adult child, no matter
how much you think it would be better for him to move out."
—MALLORY ORTBERG

• • •

"It helps parents to feel better if we remind them of our
failures with them! And how they turned out just fine despite
our imperfections. . . . We never get over needing nurturing
parents. The more we comfort our own adult children,
the more they can comfort our grandchildren."
—EDA LESHAN

• • •

"Children and mothers never truly part, bound together
by the beating of one another's heart."
—CHARLOTTE GRAY

• • •

"Kids don't stay with you if you do it right. It's the one job
where, the better you are, the more surely you won't be
needed in the long run."
—BARBARA KINGSOLVER

• • •

"When your mother asks, 'Do you want a piece of advice?'
It is a mere formality. It doesn't matter if you answer yes or no.
You're going to get it anyway."
—ERMA BOMBECK

• • •

"Mothers never retire, no matter how old her children are she is always a Mom, always willing to encourage and help her children in any way she can!"
—CATHERINE PULSIFER

• • •

"With grown children, we can look back at both our mistakes and what we did well in our parenting, having conversations with a greater degree of honesty than was possible before. In getting older themselves, our adult children may begin to comprehend the burdens and strengths we carried from our own parents."
—WENDY LUSTBADER

• • •

"It really doesn't matter what age or stage a mother is at.
Once you're a mother, you're a mother forever."
—Rebecca Barlow Jordan, *Day-votions for
Grandmothers: Heart to Heart Encouragement*

• • •

"Nothing is more debilitating than to care about something you
can't do anything about. And you can't do anything about your
adult children. You can want better for them, and maybe even
begin to provide something for them, but in the long run, you
cannot do anything about someone else's vibration other than
hold them in the best light you can, mentally, and then project
that to them. And sometimes, distance makes that much more
possible than being up close to them."
—Esther Hicks

• • •

9

A Tribe Called Motherhood

"Behind every successful mama is a tribe of other mamas who have her back."
—Good Mother Project

• • •

"As parents we're meant to help each other out and build each other up."
—Galit Breen, *Kindness Wins*

• • •

"Go out and find your tribe to expand your 'family.' Don't be afraid to speak your truth to find out just who your tribe really is—they are the best investment for your mental wellbeing. Once you find them, support them when possible and ask for the same in return when you need help."
—AMBER SIMS HINTERPLATTNER, MOTHER, HEALTH-CHOICE ADVOCATE, AND AWARD-WINNING ENTREPRENEUR

• • •

"It takes a village to raise a child."
—AFRICAN PROVERB

• • •

"Joining a tribe of women who know the sacrifice, joy, beauty, and difficulties of motherhood is an incredible gift to cherish."
—MEGAN GILGER, *THE FRESH EXCHANGE*

• • •

"Mothers, daughters, and their daughters too.
Woman to woman
We're singin' with you."
—"SISTERS ARE DOIN' IT FOR THEMSELVES" BY ARETHA
FRANKLIN AND EURYTHMICS

• • •

"Differences don't matter when you have being a
mom in common."
—JOSEPHINE HAUSER, *THE STYLE HOSTESS*

• • •

"When I was a new mom, that's when I started to find my real
friends. My mom tribe. It was then that life took it upon itself to
weed out the 'acquaintances' from the friends and I couldn't be
more grateful for the strong group of women I was left with."
—BECKY MANSFIELD, *YOUR MODERN FAMILY*

• • •

"Associating with other moms is a vital lifeline to our
sanity and our sense of humor."
—SUSAN WINTER

• • •

"When you've become a mom, the simple truth is that
you might need friends who know how to change a diaper
with one hand while holding a toddler back with the other,
lest they jump into the sh*tty pile."
—MARIE SOUTHARD OSPINA

• • •

"As moms, we are in it together - raising the future. We are a tribe
of future makers. So let's support each other."
—MARISSA HERMER

• • •

"No matter what country we live in, where we reside, what we believe, our backgrounds, and our education, or faith, we women should together embrace, lift each other up, and reach out to the marginalized and less privileged."
—Dr. Jeanette Pinto, former Principal of Sophia College and author of *Wonder Women of India*

• • •

"And when you find that tribe? Hold on tight. They will be your lifeline and will make mothering those babies just a little bit easier."
—Karen Liszewski, *Motherhood Uncluttered*

• • •

"You will be too much for some people. Those aren't your people."
—Glennon Doyle

• • •

"The women in the room chatted about love, about childhood, about losing parents, about Mr. Spock, about good books they'd read. They mothered each other."
—Louise Penny, *Bury Your Dead*

• • •

"You and I aren't likely to experience what it's like to raise children in an actual village, but that's okay. That's not what this generation is about. This generation is about waking up to who we really are and what we really want, and resetting society's sails accordingly. Playing your part in the re-villaging of our culture starts with being wholly, unapologetically, courageously YOU."
—Beth Berry of *Revolution From Home* in an article written for *Motherly*

• • •

"As daughters of our Heavenly Father, and as daughters of Eve, we are all mothers and we have always been mothers. And we each have the responsibility to love and help lead the rising generation."
—SHERI L. DEW

• • •

"Wherever in the world you live, if you are a mom you have a built-in sisterhood of mothers everywhere. The experiences and circumstances of each mom may vary widely, but what every mom shares is a love for her child that is unsurpassed, and a desire to raise a happy, healthy child."
—JENNIFER WALDBURGER AND JILL SPIVACK, *SLEEPY PLANET PARENTING*

• • •

"Find your tribe. Love them hard."
—DANIELLE LAPORTE

• • •

"One thing I have learned is that the mothers who are kind and friendly, who love my kids, who speak respectfully about others, include everyone; those are my people."
—JANINE NYQUIST

• • •

"When you have a close friend you're saying, 'Your life will not go unnoticed because I will notice it. Your life will not go unwitnessed because I will be your witness.'"
—DR. SHERYL ZIEGLER

• • •

"My sisters eat, laugh, scold each other, and sing together. They are the keepers of the deepest of mommy secrets. They are the stewards of the motherships in the darkest of nights. These mothers are my sisters for life."
—SHANA SWAIN FOR *HuffPost*

• • •

"My tribe saved me. Without these women and their families, I feel very strongly that I would have fallen into that dark place on which I teetered again and again in my journey, and I'm not so sure I would have resurfaced."
—Hannah Spray for *Green Moms Collective*

• • •

"Find a group of people who challenge and inspire you; spend a lot of time with them, and it will change your life."
—Amy Poehler

• • •

"It's helpful to have friends who completely understand that movie night at our place now needs to start after the baby is in bed. They send invites that say "babies welcome :)." Our baby is not an inconvenience because they are dealing with the same constraints, so we all figure it out as we go. 'Friends who are moms' basically picked up the same hobby as I did, at the same time, and now we all do it together."
—by Rebecca Shamblin for *Ravishly*

• • •

Conclusion

Thank you for joining me on this journey to honor the mothers in our lives. From thoughts on the life-changing journey of motherhood to our mothers as life source; from honoring the unique place our mothers hold in our lives, to saluting the fierce mama bears in our midst, I hope you found inspiring words that resonated with your spirit.

—Carissa Bonham

Photo credit: Lindsey Wiatt Photography

About the Author

Carissa Bonham lives near Portland, Oregon, with a house full of boys and a yard full of chickens. She is an award-winning writer for her work on her green and non-toxic lifestyle blog, *Creative Green Living*, where she teaches families how to make healthier choices that are beautiful, delicious, and really work.

Carissa advocates for kids and families both locally and in the Oregon state legislature. In 2019, she cut her work hours by 90 percent to spend time fighting back against HB3063 —a bill which would have discriminated against kids for medical and religious differences.

When she isn't fighting government corruption and discrimination against families, you might find her teaching local classes, making informative Facebook lives (as both Creative Green Living and Carissa Bonham), attending school board meetings, or just playing at the park with her kids.

Acknowledgments

Nobody writes a book alone —and this book especially. The vast majority of the words on these pages are not my own: They are wisdom shared by or about our foremothers. Without the individual quoted authors' desire to share, this book obviously would not have been possible.

I would like to thank the women in my family from my own mother, Lynanne, and my "bonus mom," Michelle, as well as my grandmothers, Marjorie and Marie, and "little" sister, Cambria, who each entered her journey to motherhood before I did. Growing up with such amazing women who poured into my life helped me experience motherhood differently than I would have otherwise.

I would also like to thank my assistant, Briana, who helped me find, vet, and source-check quotes for this book. I'm sure she's as glad as I am to see this project complete and in print. She was indispensable for this project and I am so grateful to have her on my team.

A thank-you is also due to my editor at Skyhorse, Nicole Frail. A mother herself, Nicole and I have now worked on three books together. If she hadn't taken a chance on a blogger with a pretty Instagram feed four years ago, there are so many opportunities I would have missed! Thanks, Nicole.

The final acknowledgement I would like to give is to the fierce mama bears who found their voices and rose to speak truth to power in order to fight for their kids in 2019. While similar movements happened across the United States that year, I was intensely involved in the fight for the educational access rights of medical and religious minorities in Oregon during the 2019 legislative session. The brilliant, dedicated, and generous mothers I met during this time were a true inspiration and living testimony of what happens when we all bring our gifts to the table to work for a greater purpose.

The warrior moms who faced a similar battle in California were no less inspiring, and I watched many Facebook Lives and followed along on social media with tears running down my face as mothers placed their bodies on the line in peaceful protest as they stood to defend their kids. These events happened at the same time I was working on this book, which is dedicated to them and their inspiring courage.

Index